Daily & Weekly Planner

_____

_____

All rights reserved. No part of this book may be reproduced in any form by any electronic or mechanical means including photocopying, recording, or information storage and retrieval without permission in writing from the author.

Printed by CreateSpace, An Amazon.com Company
A Publication by Undated Daily Planner

Important Dates

Important Dates

Notes

Notes

Month: ………………………………….Year: ………………………….

Time	Sunday	Monday	Tuesday	Wednesday
8 AM				
10 AM				
12 PM				
2 PM				
4 PM				
6 PM				
8 PM				
10 PM				
Notes				

Month: ....Year: ....

Time	Thursday	Friday	Saturday	To do list
8 AM				
10 AM				
12 PM				
2 PM				
4 PM				
6 PM				
8 PM				
10 PM				
Notes				

Month: ………………………………..Year: ………………………

Time	Sunday	Monday	Tuesday	Wednesday
8 AM				
10 AM				
12 PM				
2 PM				
4 PM				
6 PM				
8 PM				
10 PM				
Notes				

Month: ……………………………………..Year: ………………………….

Time	Thursday	Friday	Saturday	To do list
8 AM				
10 AM				
12 PM				
2 PM				
4 PM				
6 PM				
8 PM				
10 PM				
Notes				

Month: ……………………………… Year: ………………………

Time	Sunday	Monday	Tuesday	Wednesday
8 AM				
10 AM				
12 PM				
2 PM				
4 PM				
6 PM				
8 PM				
10 PM				
Notes				

Month: ……………………………… Year: ………………………

Time	Thursday	Friday	Saturday	To do list
8 AM				
10 AM				
12 PM				
2 PM				
4 PM				
6 PM				
8 PM				
10 PM				
Notes				

Month: ……………………………………….Year: …………………………

Time	Sunday	Monday	Tuesday	Wednesday
8 AM				
10 AM				
12 PM				
2 PM				
4 PM				
6 PM				
8 PM				
10 PM				
Notes				

Month: .... Year: ....

Time	Thursday	Friday	Saturday	To do list
8 AM				
10 AM				
12 PM				
2 PM				
4 PM				
6 PM				
8 PM				
10 PM				
Notes				

Month: ……………………………….Year: ………………………

Time	Sunday	Monday	Tuesday	Wednesday
8 AM				
10 AM				
12 PM				
2 PM				
4 PM				
6 PM				
8 PM				
10 PM				
Notes				

Month: ………………………………….Year: ………………………….

Time	Thursday	Friday	Saturday	To do list
8 AM				
10 AM				
12 PM				
2 PM				
4 PM				
6 PM				
8 PM				
10 PM				
Notes				

Month: ……………………………………..Year: ………………………….

Time	Sunday	Monday	Tuesday	Wednesday
8 AM				
10 AM				
12 PM				
2 PM				
4 PM				
6 PM				
8 PM				
10 PM				
Notes				

Month: ……………………………… Year: ………………………

Time	Thursday	Friday	Saturday	To do list
8 AM				
10 AM				
12 PM				
2 PM				
4 PM				
6 PM				
8 PM				
10 PM				
Notes				

Month: ……………………………………….Year: ………………………………

Time	Sunday	Monday	Tuesday	Wednesday
8 AM				
10 AM				
12 PM				
2 PM				
4 PM				
6 PM				
8 PM				
10 PM				
Notes				

Month: ……………………………………….Year: ………………………….

Time	Thursday	Friday	Saturday	To do list
8 AM				
10 AM				
12 PM				
2 PM				
4 PM				
6 PM				
8 PM				
10 PM				
Notes				

Month: ……………………………………..Year: ………………………….

Time	Sunday	Monday	Tuesday	Wednesday
8 AM				
10 AM				
12 PM				
2 PM				
4 PM				
6 PM				
8 PM				
10 PM				
Notes				

Month: ……………………………………….Year: …………………………….

Time	Thursday	Friday	Saturday	To do list
8 AM				
10 AM				
12 PM				
2 PM				
4 PM				
6 PM				
8 PM				
10 PM				
Notes				

Month: ……………………………………….Year: ……………………….

Time	Sunday	Monday	Tuesday	Wednesday
8 AM				
10 AM				
12 PM				
2 PM				
4 PM				
6 PM				
8 PM				
10 PM				
Notes				

Month: ……………………………………. Year: ……………………………

Time	Thursday	Friday	Saturday	To do list
8 AM				
10 AM				
12 PM				
2 PM				
4 PM				
6 PM				
8 PM				
10 PM				
Notes				

Month: ……………………………….Year: ……………………….

Time	Sunday	Monday	Tuesday	Wednesday
8 AM				
10 AM				
12 PM				
2 PM				
4 PM				
6 PM				
8 PM				
10 PM				
Notes				

Month: ……………………………………Year: …………………………………

Time	Thursday	Friday	Saturday	To do list
8 AM				
10 AM				
12 PM				
2 PM				
4 PM				
6 PM				
8 PM				
10 PM				
Notes				

Month: ……………………………….Year: ………………………….

Time	Sunday	Monday	Tuesday	Wednesday
8 AM				
10 AM				
12 PM				
2 PM				
4 PM				
6 PM				
8 PM				
10 PM				
Notes				

Month: ……………………………….Year: …………………………

Time	Thursday	Friday	Saturday	To do list
8 AM				
10 AM				
12 PM				
2 PM				
4 PM				
6 PM				
8 PM				
10 PM				
Notes				

Month: ………………………………….Year: ………………………….

Time	Sunday	Monday	Tuesday	Wednesday
8 AM				
10 AM				
12 PM				
2 PM				
4 PM				
6 PM				
8 PM				
10 PM				
Notes				

Month: ……………………………………..Year: ………………………….

Time	Thursday	Friday	Saturday	To do list
8 AM				
10 AM				
12 PM				
2 PM				
4 PM				
6 PM				
8 PM				
10 PM				
Notes				

Month: …………………………………….Year: ………………………….

Time	Sunday	Monday	Tuesday	Wednesday
8 AM				
10 AM				
12 PM				
2 PM				
4 PM				
6 PM				
8 PM				
10 PM				
Notes				

Month: ……………………………………Year: ……………………………

Time	Thursday	Friday	Saturday	**To do list**
8 AM				
10 AM				
12 PM				
2 PM				
4 PM				
6 PM				
8 PM				
10 PM				
Notes				

Month: ……………………………………….Year: ………………………………

Time	Sunday	Monday	Tuesday	Wednesday
8 AM				
10 AM				
12 PM				
2 PM				
4 PM				
6 PM				
8 PM				
10 PM				
Notes				

Month: ……………………………………….Year: ………………………….

Time	Thursday	Friday	Saturday	To do list
8 AM				
10 AM				
12 PM				
2 PM				
4 PM				
6 PM				
8 PM				
10 PM				
Notes				

Month: ……………………………………..Year: …………………………..

Time	Sunday	Monday	Tuesday	Wednesday
8 AM				
10 AM				
12 PM				
2 PM				
4 PM				
6 PM				
8 PM				
10 PM				
Notes				

Month: ……………………………….Year: ………………………

Time	Thursday	Friday	Saturday	To do list
8 AM				
10 AM				
12 PM				
2 PM				
4 PM				
6 PM				
8 PM				
10 PM				
Notes				

Month: ……………………………….Year: ……………………….

Time	Sunday	Monday	Tuesday	Wednesday
8 AM				
10 AM				
12 PM				
2 PM				
4 PM				
6 PM				
8 PM				
10 PM				
Notes				

Month: ……………………………… Year: …………………………

Time	Thursday	Friday	Saturday	To do list
8 AM				
10 AM				
12 PM				
2 PM				
4 PM				
6 PM				
8 PM				
10 PM				
Notes				

Month: ……………………………………..Year: ………………………….

Time	Sunday	Monday	Tuesday	Wednesday
8 AM				
10 AM				
12 PM				
2 PM				
4 PM				
6 PM				
8 PM				
10 PM				
Notes				

Month: ……………………………………….Year: ………………………….

Time	Thursday	Friday	Saturday	To do list
8 AM				
10 AM				
12 PM				
2 PM				
4 PM				
6 PM				
8 PM				
10 PM				
Notes				

Month: ……………………………………….Year: ………………………….

Time	Sunday	Monday	Tuesday	Wednesday
8 AM				
10 AM				
12 PM				
2 PM				
4 PM				
6 PM				
8 PM				
10 PM				
Notes				

Month: ……………………………………….Year: ………………………….

Time	Thursday	Friday	Saturday	To do list
8 AM				
10 AM				
12 PM				
2 PM				
4 PM				
6 PM				
8 PM				
10 PM				
Notes				

Month: ……………………………………..Year: ………………………….

Time	Sunday	Monday	Tuesday	Wednesday
8 AM				
10 AM				
12 PM				
2 PM				
4 PM				
6 PM				
8 PM				
10 PM				
Notes				

Month: ………………………………….Year: ……………………….

Time	Thursday	Friday	Saturday	To do list
8 AM				
10 AM				
12 PM				
2 PM				
4 PM				
6 PM				
8 PM				
10 PM				
Notes				

Month: ……………………………………..Year: ………………………….

Time	Sunday	Monday	Tuesday	Wednesday
8 AM				
10 AM				
12 PM				
2 PM				
4 PM				
6 PM				
8 PM				
10 PM				
Notes				

Month: ………………………………….Year: ………………………

Time	Thursday	Friday	Saturday	To do list
8 AM				
10 AM				
12 PM				
2 PM				
4 PM				
6 PM				
8 PM				
10 PM				
Notes				

Month: ……………………………………..Year: ………………………….

Time	Sunday	Monday	Tuesday	Wednesday
8 AM				
10 AM				
12 PM				
2 PM				
4 PM				
6 PM				
8 PM				
10 PM				
Notes				

Month: ……………………………………….Year: …………………………

Time	Thursday	Friday	Saturday	To do list
8 AM				
10 AM				
12 PM				
2 PM				
4 PM				
6 PM				
8 PM				
10 PM				
Notes				

Month: ………………………………….Year: ……………………….

Time	Sunday	Monday	Tuesday	Wednesday
8 AM				
10 AM				
12 PM				
2 PM				
4 PM				
6 PM				
8 PM				
10 PM				
Notes				

Month: ....Year: ....

Time	Thursday	Friday	Saturday	To do list
8 AM				
10 AM				
12 PM				
2 PM				
4 PM				
6 PM				
8 PM				
10 PM				
Notes				

Month: ……………………………………..Year: ………………………….

Time	Sunday	Monday	Tuesday	Wednesday
8 AM				
10 AM				
12 PM				
2 PM				
4 PM				
6 PM				
8 PM				
10 PM				
Notes				

Month: ……………………………………… Year: ……………………………

Time	Thursday	Friday	Saturday	To do list
8 AM				
10 AM				
12 PM				
2 PM				
4 PM				
6 PM				
8 PM				
10 PM				
Notes				

Month: ………………………………….Year: ………………………….

Time	Sunday	Monday	Tuesday	Wednesday
8 AM				
10 AM				
12 PM				
2 PM				
4 PM				
6 PM				
8 PM				
10 PM				
Notes				

Month: ………………………………….Year: …………………………

Time	Thursday	Friday	Saturday	To do list
8 AM				
10 AM				
12 PM				
2 PM				
4 PM				
6 PM				
8 PM				
10 PM				
Notes				

Month: ……………………………………….Year: ………………………….

Time	Sunday	Monday	Tuesday	Wednesday
8 AM				
10 AM				
12 PM				
2 PM				
4 PM				
6 PM				
8 PM				
10 PM				
Notes				

Month: .... Year: ....

Time	Thursday	Friday	Saturday	To do list
8 AM				
10 AM				
12 PM				
2 PM				
4 PM				
6 PM				
8 PM				
10 PM				
Notes				

Month: ....Year: ....

Time	Sunday	Monday	Tuesday	Wednesday
8 AM				
10 AM				
12 PM				
2 PM				
4 PM				
6 PM				
8 PM				
10 PM				
Notes				

Month: ……………………………………….Year: …………………………

Time	Thursday	Friday	Saturday	To do list
8 AM				
10 AM				
12 PM				
2 PM				
4 PM				
6 PM				
8 PM				
10 PM				
Notes				

Month: ……………………………………….Year: ……………………………

Time	Sunday	Monday	Tuesday	Wednesday
8 AM				
10 AM				
12 PM				
2 PM				
4 PM				
6 PM				
8 PM				
10 PM				
Notes				

Month: .... Year: ....

Time	Thursday	Friday	Saturday	To do list
8 AM				
10 AM				
12 PM				
2 PM				
4 PM				
6 PM				
8 PM				
10 PM				
Notes				

Month: ……………………………………..Year: …………………………

Time	Sunday	Monday	Tuesday	Wednesday
8 AM				
10 AM				
12 PM				
2 PM				
4 PM				
6 PM				
8 PM				
10 PM				
Notes				

Month: ……………………………………Year: ………………………….

Time	Thursday	Friday	Saturday	To do list
8 AM				
10 AM				
12 PM				
2 PM				
4 PM				
6 PM				
8 PM				
10 PM				
Notes				

Month: ……………………………………..Year: …………………………….

Time	Sunday	Monday	Tuesday	Wednesday
8 AM				
10 AM				
12 PM				
2 PM				
4 PM				
6 PM				
8 PM				
10 PM				
Notes				

Month: .... Year: ....

Time	Thursday	Friday	Saturday	To do list
8 AM				
10 AM				
12 PM				
2 PM				
4 PM				
6 PM				
8 PM				
10 PM				
Notes				

Month: ……………………………….Year: ……………………….

Time	Sunday	Monday	Tuesday	Wednesday
8 AM				
10 AM				
12 PM				
2 PM				
4 PM				
6 PM				
8 PM				
10 PM				
Notes				

Month: ……………………………………….Year: …………………………

Time	Thursday	Friday	Saturday	To do list
8 AM				
10 AM				
12 PM				
2 PM				
4 PM				
6 PM				
8 PM				
10 PM				
Notes				

Month: ……………………………………….Year: ……………………………

Time	Sunday	Monday	Tuesday	Wednesday
8 AM				
10 AM				
12 PM				
2 PM				
4 PM				
6 PM				
8 PM				
10 PM				
Notes				

Month: ……………………………….Year: ………………………

Time	Thursday	Friday	Saturday	To do list
8 AM				
10 AM				
12 PM				
2 PM				
4 PM				
6 PM				
8 PM				
10 PM				
Notes				

Month: ……………………………………..Year: ………………………….

Time	Sunday	Monday	Tuesday	Wednesday
8 AM				
10 AM				
12 PM				
2 PM				
4 PM				
6 PM				
8 PM				
10 PM				
Notes				

Month: ………………………………….Year: ………………………

Time	Thursday	Friday	Saturday	To do list
8 AM				
10 AM				
12 PM				
2 PM				
4 PM				
6 PM				
8 PM				
10 PM				
Notes				

Month: ....Year: ....

Time	Sunday	Monday	Tuesday	Wednesday
8 AM				
10 AM				
12 PM				
2 PM				
4 PM				
6 PM				
8 PM				
10 PM				
Notes				

Month: ……………………………………….Year: ……………………………

Time	Thursday	Friday	Saturday	To do list
8 AM				
10 AM				
12 PM				
2 PM				
4 PM				
6 PM				
8 PM				
10 PM				
Notes				

Month: ……………………………………..Year: ………………………….

Time	Sunday	Monday	Tuesday	Wednesday
8 AM				
10 AM				
12 PM				
2 PM				
4 PM				
6 PM				
8 PM				
10 PM				
Notes				

Month: ……………………………………. Year: …………………………

Time	Thursday	Friday	Saturday	To do list
8 AM				
10 AM				
12 PM				
2 PM				
4 PM				
6 PM				
8 PM				
10 PM				
Notes				

Month: ……………………………………….Year: ……………………………….

Time	Sunday	Monday	Tuesday	Wednesday
8 AM				
10 AM				
12 PM				
2 PM				
4 PM				
6 PM				
8 PM				
10 PM				
Notes				

Month: ……………………………………. Year: ………………………….

Time	Thursday	Friday	Saturday	To do list
8 AM				
10 AM				
12 PM				
2 PM				
4 PM				
6 PM				
8 PM				
10 PM				
Notes				

Month: ……………………………………….Year: ………………………….

Time	Sunday	Monday	Tuesday	Wednesday
8 AM				
10 AM				
12 PM				
2 PM				
4 PM				
6 PM				
8 PM				
10 PM				
Notes				

Month: ……………………………………….Year: …………………………

Time	Thursday	Friday	Saturday	To do list
8 AM				
10 AM				
12 PM				
2 PM				
4 PM				
6 PM				
8 PM				
10 PM				
Notes				

Month: ....Year: ....

Time	Sunday	Monday	Tuesday	Wednesday
8 AM				
10 AM				
12 PM				
2 PM				
4 PM				
6 PM				
8 PM				
10 PM				
Notes				

Month: ……………………………….Year: ………………………….

Time	Thursday	Friday	Saturday	To do list
8 AM				
10 AM				
12 PM				
2 PM				
4 PM				
6 PM				
8 PM				
10 PM				
Notes				

Month: ……………………………….Year: ……………………….

Time	Sunday	Monday	Tuesday	Wednesday
8 AM				
10 AM				
12 PM				
2 PM				
4 PM				
6 PM				
8 PM				
10 PM				
Notes				

Month: ………………………………….Year: …………………….

Time	Thursday	Friday	Saturday	**To do list**
8 AM				
10 AM				
12 PM				
2 PM				
4 PM				
6 PM				
8 PM				
10 PM				
Notes				

Month: ……………………………….Year: ………………………

Time	Sunday	Monday	Tuesday	Wednesday
8 AM				
10 AM				
12 PM				
2 PM				
4 PM				
6 PM				
8 PM				
10 PM				
Notes				

Month: ……………………………………… Year: ………………………………

Time	Thursday	Friday	Saturday	To do list
8 AM				
10 AM				
12 PM				
2 PM				
4 PM				
6 PM				
8 PM				
10 PM				
Notes				

Month: ……………………………………….Year: ………………………….

Time	Sunday	Monday	Tuesday	Wednesday
8 AM				
10 AM				
12 PM				
2 PM				
4 PM				
6 PM				
8 PM				
10 PM				
Notes				

Month: ……………………………………..Year: ………………………….

Time	Thursday	Friday	Saturday	To do list
8 AM				
10 AM				
12 PM				
2 PM				
4 PM				
6 PM				
8 PM				
10 PM				
Notes				

Month: ……………………………….Year: ………………………….

Time	Sunday	Monday	Tuesday	Wednesday
8 AM				
10 AM				
12 PM				
2 PM				
4 PM				
6 PM				
8 PM				
10 PM				
Notes				

Month: ……………………………………….Year: ………………………………

Time	Thursday	Friday	Saturday	To do list
8 AM				
10 AM				
12 PM				
2 PM				
4 PM				
6 PM				
8 PM				
10 PM				
Notes				

Month: ……………………………….Year: ………………………….

Time	Sunday	Monday	Tuesday	Wednesday
8 AM				
10 AM				
12 PM				
2 PM				
4 PM				
6 PM				
8 PM				
10 PM				
Notes				

Month: ……………………………………. Year: ………………………………

Time	Thursday	Friday	Saturday	To do list
8 AM				
10 AM				
12 PM				
2 PM				
4 PM				
6 PM				
8 PM				
10 PM				
Notes				

Month: ……………………………………..Year: …………………………..

Time	Sunday	Monday	Tuesday	Wednesday
8 AM				
10 AM				
12 PM				
2 PM				
4 PM				
6 PM				
8 PM				
10 PM				
Notes				

Month: ....Year: ....

Time	Thursday	Friday	Saturday	To do list
8 AM				
10 AM				
12 PM				
2 PM				
4 PM				
6 PM				
8 PM				
10 PM				
Notes				

Month: ……………………………….Year: ………………………

Time	Sunday	Monday	Tuesday	Wednesday
8 AM				
10 AM				
12 PM				
2 PM				
4 PM				
6 PM				
8 PM				
10 PM				
Notes				

Month: ……………………………………….Year: ……………………………

Time	Thursday	Friday	Saturday	To do list
8 AM				
10 AM				
12 PM				
2 PM				
4 PM				
6 PM				
8 PM				
10 PM				
Notes				

Month: ……………………………….Year: ………………………..

Time	Sunday	Monday	Tuesday	Wednesday
8 AM				
10 AM				
12 PM				
2 PM				
4 PM				
6 PM				
8 PM				
10 PM				
Notes				

Month: ………………………………….Year: ………………………….

Time	Thursday	Friday	Saturday	To do list
8 AM				
10 AM				
12 PM				
2 PM				
4 PM				
6 PM				
8 PM				
10 PM				
Notes				

Month: ……………………………………Year: ………………………….

Time	Sunday	Monday	Tuesday	Wednesday
8 AM				
10 AM				
12 PM				
2 PM				
4 PM				
6 PM				
8 PM				
10 PM				
Notes				

Month: ……………………………………. Year: …………………………

Time	Thursday	Friday	Saturday	To do list
8 AM				
10 AM				
12 PM				
2 PM				
4 PM				
6 PM				
8 PM				
10 PM				
Notes				

Month: ……………………………………..Year: ………………………….

Time	Sunday	Monday	Tuesday	Wednesday
8 AM				
10 AM				
12 PM				
2 PM				
4 PM				
6 PM				
8 PM				
10 PM				
Notes				

Month: ……………………………………. Year: …………………………

Time	Thursday	Friday	Saturday	To do list
8 AM				
10 AM				
12 PM				
2 PM				
4 PM				
6 PM				
8 PM				
10 PM				
Notes				

Month: …………………………………….Year: ………………………….

Time	Sunday	Monday	Tuesday	Wednesday
8 AM				
10 AM				
12 PM				
2 PM				
4 PM				
6 PM				
8 PM				
10 PM				
Notes				

Month: ……………………………………….. Year: …………………………….

Time	Thursday	Friday	Saturday	To do list
8 AM				
10 AM				
12 PM				
2 PM				
4 PM				
6 PM				
8 PM				
10 PM				
Notes				

Month: ………………………………….Year: ………………………….

Time	Sunday	Monday	Tuesday	Wednesday
8 AM				
10 AM				
12 PM				
2 PM				
4 PM				
6 PM				
8 PM				
10 PM				
Notes				

Month: ....Year: ....

Time	Thursday	Friday	Saturday	To do list
8 AM				
10 AM				
12 PM				
2 PM				
4 PM				
6 PM				
8 PM				
10 PM				
Notes				

Month: ……………………………….Year: ………………………..

Time	Sunday	Monday	Tuesday	Wednesday
8 AM				
10 AM				
12 PM				
2 PM				
4 PM				
6 PM				
8 PM				
10 PM				
Notes				

Month: ....Year: ....

Time	Thursday	Friday	Saturday	To do list
8 AM				
10 AM				
12 PM				
2 PM				
4 PM				
6 PM				
8 PM				
10 PM				
Notes				

Month: ……………………………………..Year: ………………………….

Time	Sunday	Monday	Tuesday	Wednesday
8 AM				
10 AM				
12 PM				
2 PM				
4 PM				
6 PM				
8 PM				
10 PM				
Notes				

Month: ……………………………………..Year: …………………………….

Time	Thursday	Friday	Saturday	**To do list**
8 AM				
10 AM				
12 PM				
2 PM				
4 PM				
6 PM				
8 PM				
10 PM				
Notes				

Month: ……………………………………….Year: ………………………….

Time	Sunday	Monday	Tuesday	Wednesday
8 AM				
10 AM				
12 PM				
2 PM				
4 PM				
6 PM				
8 PM				
10 PM				
Notes				

Month: ....Year: ....

Time	Thursday	Friday	Saturday	To do list
8 AM				
10 AM				
12 PM				
2 PM				
4 PM				
6 PM				
8 PM				
10 PM				
Notes				

Month: ……………………………….Year: ………………………

Time	Sunday	Monday	Tuesday	Wednesday
8 AM				
10 AM				
12 PM				
2 PM				
4 PM				
6 PM				
8 PM				
10 PM				
Notes				

Month: ………………………………….Year: ………………………

Time	Thursday	Friday	Saturday	To do list
8 AM				
10 AM				
12 PM				
2 PM				
4 PM				
6 PM				
8 PM				
10 PM				
Notes				

Month: ……………………………………..Year: ………………………..

Time	Sunday	Monday	Tuesday	Wednesday
8 AM				
10 AM				
12 PM				
2 PM				
4 PM				
6 PM				
8 PM				
10 PM				
Notes				

Month: ……………………………………. Year: ……………………………

Time	Thursday	Friday	Saturday	To do list
8 AM				
10 AM				
12 PM				
2 PM				
4 PM				
6 PM				
8 PM				
10 PM				
Notes				

Month: ……………………………………… Year: ………………………………

Time	Sunday	Monday	Tuesday	Wednesday
8 AM				
10 AM				
12 PM				
2 PM				
4 PM				
6 PM				
8 PM				
10 PM				
Notes				

Month: ……………………………….Year: ……………………….

Time	Thursday	Friday	Saturday	To do list
8 AM				
10 AM				
12 PM				
2 PM				
4 PM				
6 PM				
8 PM				
10 PM				
Notes				

Month: ……………………………………..Year: ………………………….

Time	Sunday	Monday	Tuesday	Wednesday
8 AM				
10 AM				
12 PM				
2 PM				
4 PM				
6 PM				
8 PM				
10 PM				
Notes				

Month: ……………………………………….Year: ……………………………

Time	Thursday	Friday	Saturday	To do list
8 AM				
10 AM				
12 PM				
2 PM				
4 PM				
6 PM				
8 PM				
10 PM				
Notes				

Month: ……………………………….Year: ……………………….

Time	Sunday	Monday	Tuesday	Wednesday
8 AM				
10 AM				
12 PM				
2 PM				
4 PM				
6 PM				
8 PM				
10 PM				
Notes				

Month: ……………………………………… Year: ………………………

Time	Thursday	Friday	Saturday	To do list
8 AM				
10 AM				
12 PM				
2 PM				
4 PM				
6 PM				
8 PM				
10 PM				
Notes				

Month: ………………………………….Year: ………………………….

Time	Sunday	Monday	Tuesday	Wednesday
8 AM				
10 AM				
12 PM				
2 PM				
4 PM				
6 PM				
8 PM				
10 PM				
Notes				

Month: ……………………………………… Year: ………………………………

Time	Thursday	Friday	Saturday	To do list
8 AM				
10 AM				
12 PM				
2 PM				
4 PM				
6 PM				
8 PM				
10 PM				
Notes				

Month: ……………………………………..Year: …………………………….

Time	Sunday	Monday	Tuesday	Wednesday
8 AM				
10 AM				
12 PM				
2 PM				
4 PM				
6 PM				
8 PM				
10 PM				
Notes				

Month: ……………………………………….Year: ………………………….

Time	Thursday	Friday	Saturday	To do list
8 AM				
10 AM				
12 PM				
2 PM				
4 PM				
6 PM				
8 PM				
10 PM				
Notes				

Month: ……………………………………….Year: ………………………….

Time	Sunday	Monday	Tuesday	Wednesday
8 AM				
10 AM				
12 PM				
2 PM				
4 PM				
6 PM				
8 PM				
10 PM				
Notes				

Month: .... Year: ....

Time	Thursday	Friday	Saturday	To do list
8 AM				
10 AM				
12 PM				
2 PM				
4 PM				
6 PM				
8 PM				
10 PM				
Notes				

Month: ……………………………….Year: ………………………….

Time	Sunday	Monday	Tuesday	Wednesday
8 AM				
10 AM				
12 PM				
2 PM				
4 PM				
6 PM				
8 PM				
10 PM				
Notes				

Month: ....Year: ....

Time	Thursday	Friday	**Saturday**	**To do list**
8 AM				
10 AM				
12 PM				
2 PM				
4 PM				
6 PM				
8 PM				
10 PM				
Notes				

Month: ……………………………………….Year: ………………………….

Time	Sunday	Monday	Tuesday	Wednesday
8 AM				
10 AM				
12 PM				
2 PM				
4 PM				
6 PM				
8 PM				
10 PM				
Notes				

Month: ……………………………………..Year: ……………………………

Time	Thursday	Friday	Saturday	To do list
8 AM				
10 AM				
12 PM				
2 PM				
4 PM				
6 PM				
8 PM				
10 PM				
Notes				

Month: ………………………………..Year: ……………………….

Time	Sunday	Monday	Tuesday	Wednesday
8 AM				
10 AM				
12 PM				
2 PM				
4 PM				
6 PM				
8 PM				
10 PM				
Notes				

Month: ……………………………………… Year: ………………………………

Time	Thursday	Friday	Saturday	To do list
8 AM				
10 AM				
12 PM				
2 PM				
4 PM				
6 PM				
8 PM				
10 PM				
Notes				

Month: ……………………………………….Year: …………………………….

Time	Sunday	Monday	Tuesday	Wednesday
8 AM				
10 AM				
12 PM				
2 PM				
4 PM				
6 PM				
8 PM				
10 PM				
Notes				

Month: ……………………………………….Year: ………………………….

Time	Thursday	Friday	Saturday	To do list
8 AM				
10 AM				
12 PM				
2 PM				
4 PM				
6 PM				
8 PM				
10 PM				
Notes				

Monthly

Month: ....Year:......................

Month: ....Year:......................

Month: ....Year:......................

Month: ....Year:......................

Month: ....Year:......................

Month: ....Year:......................

Month: ………………………………………Year:…………………

Month: ....Year:......................

Month: ....Year:.....................

Month: ....Year:......................

Month: ....Year:......................

Month: ....Year:.......................

Month: ………………………………………Year:…………………

Month: ....Year:......................

Month: ....Year:.....................

Month: ....Year:......................

Manufactured by Amazon.ca
Bolton, ON

30875901R00090